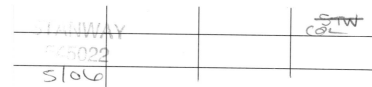

James
PARNELL
1636 – 1656

A Quaker preacher who
died in Colchester Castle

Rosalind Kaye
on behalf of Colchester Quaker Meeting

Quak
350 Y.
IN COLCHESTER

Published on the occasion of the celebration of

> # JAMES PARNELL
> ## Quaker
> ### Imprisoned for his faith & died here 1656, aged 19

Plaque in Colchester Castle

Published by
COLCHESTER QUAKER MEETING
© Colchester Quaker Meeting, 2006
ISBN 0-9552622-0-8
978-0-9552622-0-3

Designed and typeset by Buffey & Buffey,
Coggeshall, Essex

James Parnell

A small plaque in the entrance to Colchester Castle commemorates James Parnell, the young Quaker preacher who died there in the seventeenth century. The same name appears on the list of Colchester Martyrs in the Town Hall. Who was this young man and why did he make such an impression on the history of the town?

James was born to Thomas and Sarah Parnell in Retford, Nottinghamshire, on 6 September 1636 and baptised in St Swithun's Church. He was slight of build, even when fully grown. He received a good education, probably at the Edward VIth Grammar School in the town, and acquired a thorough knowledge of the Bible. Afterwards he followed his father's trade, but the nature of this is not known.

St Swithun's Church, Retford.

England was on the verge of Civil War as James reached six years of age so he grew up during a period of political and religious unrest. By the time he entered his teens, the execution of the King and the changes in the Church had allowed radical religious ideas to be aired in public, and many new sects had been formed.

Looking back on his youth, James recalled that he had been as wild as other boys but later had had a change of heart which lead him to seek spiritual guidance. Feeling disillusioned by the local clergy, he turned elsewhere. A few miles away he found a group of like-minded people which he joined as they sat down together to wait in silent worship. Before long he heard of George Fox, the founder of Quakers, whom he determined to visit.

Fox, born in 1624 in Fenny Drayton, Leicestershire, had been a serious, God-fearing young man who had been shocked by the contrast between religious profession and moral behaviour. He spent four years travelling, discussing, reading and seeking spiritual guidance until finally, at his wits' end, he realized that 'There is one, even Jesus Christ, that can speak to thy condition'. He knew this was the answer to his search, and felt moved to share his insights with others, first in neighbouring counties and then further afield.

Fox preached the priority of the spirit over the letter of the law. He believed that everyone had received a measure of the Light of God in their conscience which, if followed, would lead them to the Light of Life, without the intervention of clergy; the Bible was his chief guide. Although his ideas were not original, for they can be traced in earlier writings, he had great authority which sprang from his depth of insight and a profound conviction of the reality of his experience. His unusual stamina carried him through forty years of travel, preaching and imprisonment. 'While I was in the dungeon at Carlisle' he wrote in his Journal, 'James Parnell, a little lad of about sixteen years of age came to see me and was convinced.'

James returned home to resume his trade but his conviction grew, to the dismay of his family. He travelled south a few miles to meet a group of people who were already worshipping together. While there he felt called to go to Cambridge where two Quakers had been whipped for denouncing the

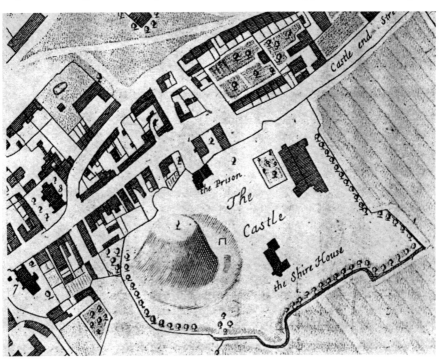

Loggan's plan of Cambridge Castle showing the prison in 1688.

deceit they saw around them. He knew that he might suffer in the same way for he was bringing the same message; however he was met by some of the townspeople who were sympathetic to his cause.

Fired with the youthful certainty of his belief, James confronted those in authority. Addressing the Masters of the Colleges he challenged 'Did Abraham ever pay Tythes...?'; of the Justices he asked 'where do you ever read that Pharoah[1] King of Egypt ... did command Moses or Aaron to put off their Hats, or Fine or Imprison them if they would not ...?' and to the Magistrates, 'You have a Law against Swearers, & yet by Your Law seek to compel men to swear: ... be ashamed of your Profession'. He was arrested by the Mayor and held in the Castle prison but no charges could be found to bring against him. Eventually the Magistrate directed members of the jury to find the papers seditious and scandalous, but he was thwarted when they could find only that the papers were written by him. After three days he was beaten out of town by a mob, having been given a Pass which named him as a rogue. A sympathetic Justice rode after him and removed the Pass, setting him free.

He returned later and spent about six months preaching in the surrounding areas of Cambridgeshire, Huntingdon and the Isle of Ely. He was invited to engage in disputations with clergy and some of Baptist

[1] sic

persuasion. As well as arguments conducted in person, the breakdown of censorship allowed a 'pamphlet war' to be waged between Quakers and their detractors; James published a rebuttal of forty accusations which had been levelled against him. He was fearless in addressing the pride and oppression he saw in society: '... to that which is of God in all your Consciences I speak, which is my Witness against your Ungodly Lives; ... Fear and Dread the Lord God, and Repent'.

On leaving Cambridge, James was drawn to visit Essex where he had heard there were people searching for new light. The north of the county had a tradition of radical religious activity, having been a centre of Lollardy, and more recently, of dissatisfaction with the Church, so it was fertile ground for the Quaker message. He preached in Halstead, Stebbing, Felsted, Coggeshall and Witham; many were convinced but there was also much opposition.

Early in July 1655 he arrived in Colchester. The townspeople were already 'talking and discoursing of a people called Quakers' but Stephen Crisp (who was soon to be convinced by James's preaching) recalled 'I could hear no good report of them but much harm.'

On the following day, Sunday, James preached first in his lodgings at Thomas Shortland's house, then spoke to the congregation after the sermon

Coggeshall Church, 1832.

in St Nicholas Church (as was permitted at the time); in the afternoon he addressed a large crowd from the hay loft in John Furley's yard and finally disputed with the town Lecturer and a clergyman. He spent the rest of the week preaching in the town. Many were convinced by his message and went on to found a Quaker Meeting in the town. Others turned against him but he continued to engage them in dialogue; some resorted to physical attacks but he received these patiently.

Coggeshall Church held a Fast on 12 July to pray against the errors of the Quakers; their intention was to ensnare James and have him arrested. Knowing of their plans, James nonetheless returned to the town,

being prepared to answer for his faith. After the preacher had denounced the Quakers from the pulpit, James began to speak to the congregation but he was interrupted several times and some confusion followed. He refused to remove his hat during prayers, as requested, but instead left the Church so that he could speak to the people more freely.

On his way through the town James was arrested by Justice Wakering and questioned by a group of clergymen and magistrates who accused him of riotous behaviour and telling the Preacher that he spoke falsely. He was taken to the County Gaol in Colchester Castle and denied visitors. He wrote a reply to the charges against him, explaining why he was innocent, and sent it to the Justice.

The trial was held in Chelmsford, where James was taken in chains with other prisoners. In court he was allowed to appear without shackles, but again he refused to remove his hat when ordered to do so. The Jury accepted his reply to the charges when it was read out in court, rather than the testimony of false witnesses, and found him innocent. The Judge nonetheless fined him £40 for contempt of the Magistry and the Ministry, commanding the gaoler to take him back to prison and let no 'giddy-headed people' visit him. James refused to pay one penny of the fine, for this would have owned himself guilty, which he was not.

Back in Colchester Castle the gaoler and his wife ill-treated James and encouraged others to do the same, while preventing his friends from helping him. He was made to sleep on a damp stone floor rather than a bed, which his friends could have provided, and was forbidden to take exercise outside. George Fox wrote in his Journal 'And as I went through Colchester I went to visit James Parnell in prison, but the cruel gaoler

THE NORTH – EAST VIEW OF COLCHESTER CASTLE.

Colchester Castle, 1738.

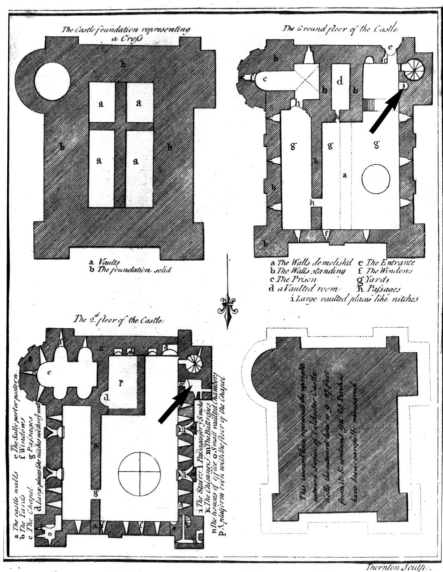

PLAN *of* **COLCHESTER CASTLE,** *in* **ESSEX.**

Plan of Colchester Castle showing where James Parnell was held.

would hardly let us come in or stay with him'. In spite of his harsh treatment James wrote letters to his friends in Essex, London and elsewhere encouraging them to continue in their faith and meet together for worship.

James was made to occupy a hole high up in the Castle wall which could only be reached by a ladder which was too short, and a rope. While returning with his food in one hand he missed the rope and fell, injuring himself badly. Friends pleaded with the gaoler to allow one of them to take his place in prison while he recovered at home, or to pay the fine, but they were refused. Everyone who saw how badly he had been injured was shocked by the way he had been treated.

When he had recovered somewhat he was put in a small airless hole. Eventually after nine months in gaol his strength declined and he took no food for ten days; a fellow prisoner later testified that James's leg had been inflamed. Finally, knowing that his end was near, he said to friends who were with him 'Here I die innocently'. He departed on 10 April 1656 and was buried in an unmarked grave in the Castle grounds because the gaoler would not release his body without fees.

At the inquest on 5 May some members of the jury used devious means to arrive at the verdict that James had contributed to his own death by fasting for ten days. While some Quakers chose to fast for religious reasons, it is more probable that James was too ill to eat. Those who were antagonistic to Quakers quickly published their account of James's death in order to influence public opinion. In answer to this, James's friends published '... *a True Testimony given concerning the Sufferings and death of James Parnell ...*' giving accounts of his ill-treatment in prison by the gaoler and his wife, and evidence submitted to the inquest.

———————

The Civil War and Interregnum was a time of comparative religious freedom, the Church Courts having been abolished, yet James Parnell was the first of many names to be written in the early book of Quaker Testimonies which recorded those who had died for their faith, even before the Restoration. Cromwell had declared himself in favour of religious toleration, but feared that complete freedom would lead to anarchy. Followers of George Fox had gathered strength in the north of England before coming south, so could not be put down as easily as some of the smaller, less well-organized sects.

The young preacher was forthright in his criticism of what he perceived to be the immoral behaviour of the clergy and magistrates; he was seen as subversive by those in authority, and arrested. But the juries of common people refused to convict him of the charges brought against him. His message was received readily by many who heard him, and from his preaching sprang a strong Quaker movement in Colchester and northeast Essex.

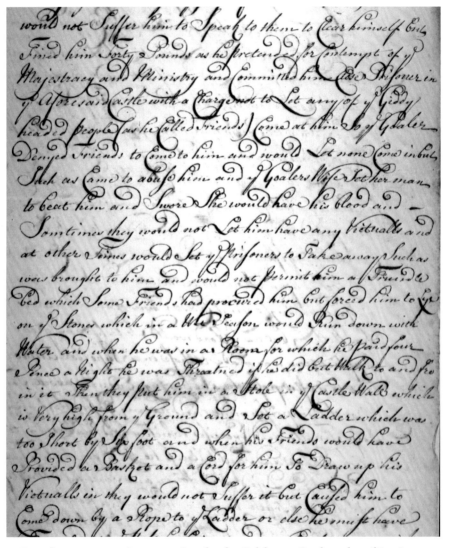

Page from a manuscript sent to London by Colchester Quakers describing James Parnell's imprisonment and death.

Sources

Parnel, James, *A Collection of the Several Writings Given forth from the Spirit of the Lord, through that Meek, Patient and Suffering Servant of God, James Parnel* (1675).

Gael, John; Coroner. Taylor, Jude; Foreman. Smith, Joseph, *A True and Lamentable Relation of the Most desperate death of James Parnel Quaker, Who willfully starved himself in the Prison of Colchester (1656).*

Talcott, Will., Shortland, Tho., *The Lambs Defence against Lyes. And a True Testimony given concerning the Sufferings and death of James Parnell, and the ground thereof.* [1656].

Fox, George, *The Journal of George Fox*, ed. J L Nickalls (1952).

Fell Smith, Charlotte, *James Parnell*, (1907).

Braithwaite, W C, *The Beginnings of Quakerism*, (1912).

Fitch, S H G, *Colchester Quakers*, (1962).

Davies, Adrian, *The Quakers in English Society*, (2000).

Moore, Rosemary, *The Light in their Consciences*, (2000)

Watts, Michael, *The Dissenters*, (1978), 1.

Illustrations

Plaque designed by Louis S M Prince, ARCA.

St Swithun's Church, Retford; by kind permission of Derbyshire County Council, from 'Picture the Past' database.

Loggan's plan of the castle yard or bailey, 1688; W M Palmer, *Cambridge Castle*, 1928.

Coggeshall Church; W Bartlett, published 1832, by kind permission of Trevor Disley, Dolphyn Framing.

View of Colchester Castle, published 1738; by kind permission of Colchester Museums.

Plan of Colchester Castle; by kind permission of Colchester Museums.

Page from a manuscript sent to London by Colchester Quakers describing James Parnell's imprisonment and death; by kind permission of the Library of the Religious Society of Friends.

Title page of James Parnell's collected works; by kind permission of Colchester Library.

A

Collection

Of the Several

WRITINGS

Given forth from the Spirit of the Lord,
through that *Meek*, *Patient* and *Suffering*
SERVANT of GOD,

James Parnel;

Who (though a Young Man) bore a Faithful
Teſtimony for God, and Dyed a Priſoner under the
Hands of a Perſecuting Generation, in *Col-
cheſter Caſtle*,, in the Year 1656.

*In the Sight of the Unwiſe they ſeemed to Dye ; and their Depar-
ture is taken for Miſery, and their going from us to be utter De-
ſtruction ; but they are in Peace : For, though they be Puniſhed
in the Sight of Men, yet is their Hope full of Immortality ; and
having been a little Chaſtized, they ſhall be greatly Rewarded ;
for, God proved them, and found them worthy for himſelf,* Wiſd.
3. 2,3,4,5. & 5. 4.
Being Dead, yet ſpeaketh, Hebr. 11. 4.

Publiſhed in the Year 1675.

Title page of James Parnell's collected works.